TIM LAHAYE

THE BIBLE'S INFLUENCE ON AMERICAN HISTORY

MASTER BOOKS

a division of CLP
San Diego, California 92115

ISBN 0-89051-018-0

Library of Congress
Catalog Card Number 76-3365

Printed in the United States of America

FOREWORD

Christian Americans are awakening to the realization that the practice of Christian principles in our national life has given way in this century to the forces of humanism and the secular state, and that for this reason our country now faces the greatest peril of its history.

On the other hand, the exciting days of the bicentennial year are witnessing a widespread renewal of interest in the Biblical foundations of America. Commensurate with this trend is a rising new interest in reclaiming America for the American idea.

What is the basic American idea? It is Christian faith and conviction arising from the Word of God and resulting in constructive action in all departments of life, including politics and government.

It is freedom, limited government, citizen responsibility, and justice for all through Bible-guided public leadership and legislation at all levels of influence, from the local neighborhood and precinct to the state and federal legislatures.

It is freedom for the people of God to rear and educate their children, share the Gospel of Christ and perform civic and political responsibilities apart from undue interference by state power.

Many of those great people who laid the foundations of America built into the fabric of this nation their own Bible-based perspective for the guidance of our political, educational and social institutions. This factor, above all, has made America unique and distinctive among the parade of nations throughout history.

A sweeping return to the will of God in our national life is long overdue. The Bible is clear in its assertion that nations which abandon the will of God shall be judged (Psalms 9:17). God declares that the rule of the wicked brings mourning to the people (Proverbs 29:2) and forces the righteous to do wrong (Psalms 125:3). Therefore, the relationship which a nation bears to the will of God as revealed in the Bible is so important as to determine its very destiny.

Dr. Tim LaHaye, renowned author, minister, and president of Christian Heritage College, is in the vanguard of prominent clergymen in America who are elevating the Word of God as the source of truth and refreshment for the nation, as well as for the church and family. In this respect Dr. LaHaye is acting very much in the American tradition.

This book testifies to Dr. LaHaye's grasp of the real essence of America, and to his desire to reclaim America for Bible-guided life, leadership, and legislation. Every Christian layman and minister in America should read this book, and it should be added to the curriculum of every Christian school.

H. Edward Rowe, President
MISSION to AMERICA

January 1, 1976

TABLE of CONTENTS

THE BIBLE'S INFLUENCE ON AMERICAN HISTORY

The GREAT AMERICAN DREAM

July 4, 1976, marks an epic birthdate for the people of the United States — the 200th anniversary of the founding of a great republic. For two hundred years we have been governed by our own elected leaders, local and national. That constitutes the longest period in human history that a free people selected its own government every four years. In such a government we have experienced unprecedented freedom, productivity, and individual responsibility. "The Great American Dream," though threatened by current humanistic philosophies that signal a departure from the principles that made us great, is still powerful enough to make this the best nation under God in which to live. Have you ever wondered what made this the greatest country in the history of the world?

1

It is no exaggeration to say that the most powerful single influence on the founding of America was the Bible. Had there been no Bible, there would be no America as we know it today! To fully grasp the accuracy of that statement, you must go back in your mind to the seventeenth century and consider the conditions that existed in Europe. Under the monarchical and feudal systems there were two kinds of people: the rulers and the ruled. A small, elite group of feudal lords, kings, governors, and dictators not only ruled the bodies and minds of the masses, but tried to control their religious consciences.

Fortunately for the Western World, the Protestant Reformation had occurred a century before, the printing press had been invented, and men like William Tyndale had translated the Bible into the tongue of the common people. As they began to read and respond to its offer of an individual relationship to God through personal salvation in Jesus Christ, they soon began to chafe against the tyranny of the ecclesiasticism in the government-controlled state church. This growing Christian movement was followed by great persecution. Puritans and separatists in England were born in such a climate, and from this the pilgrim movement began. It is well known that the Pilgrims could endure it no longer, so they migrated to Holland and then to the New World.

The MAYFLOWER PACT

In the name of God, Amen. We whose names are underwritten, the loyal subjects of our dread sovereign Lord, King James, by the grace of God, of Great Britain, France and Ireland, King, Defender of the Faith.

Having undertaken, for the glory of God and advancement of the Christian faith and honor of our King and Country, a voyage to plant the first colony in the northern parts of Virginia, do by these presents solemnly and mutually in the presence of God, and one another, covenant and combine ourselves together into a civil body politic, for our better ordering and preservation and furtherance of the ends aforesaid; and by virtue hereof to enact, constitute and frame such just and equal laws, ordinances, acts, constitutions and offices, from time to time, as shall be thought most meet and convenient for the general good of the Colony; unto which we promise all due submission and obedience.

In witness whereof we have hereunder subscribed our names at Cape Cod the 11 of November, (Nov. 21 new style calendar), in the year of the reign of our sovereign Lord, King James of England, France and Ireland the eighteenth, and of Scotland the fifty-fourth.   **Ano. Dom. 1620**

John Carver	Edward Tilly	John Goodman
William Bradford	John Tilly	Degory Prist
Edward Winslow	Francis Cooke	Thomas Williams
William Brewster	Thomas Rogers	Gilbert Winslow
Isaac Allerton	Thomas Tinker	Edmond Margeson
Myles Standish	John Rigdale	Peter Brown
John Alden	Edward Fuller	Richard Britteridge
Samuel Fuller	John Turner	George Soule
Christopher Martin	Francis Eaton	Richard Clarke
William Mullins	James Chilton	John Allerton
William White	John Crackston	Thomas English
Richard Warren	John Billington	Edward Doty
John Howland	Moses Fletcher	Edward Leister
Stephen Hopkins		

The PILGRIM and the MAYFLOWER PACT

The Pilgrim was a Biblicist with all his heart; that is, he considered the Bible as sole directory for individual and governmental behavior. He searched the Scriptures for principles, rules, mandates, and analogies to guide him in the conduct of public and private life. None can deny that his deep Christian principles founded in the Word of God inspired his quest for religious freedom, causing him to leave both England and Holland in order to establish in the New World the first New England colony.

Before leaving the ship, these Pilgrim leaders compiled the first written government document in American history. Note it carefully.

The Mayflower Pact clearly proves that its signers' primary purpose in settling this new land was "for the Glory of God and advancement of the Christian faith . . . ."

The CHARTERS

King James I, in the same year the Pilgrims arrived at Plymouth Rock, granted the New England Charter which contains the following clause:

We, according to our princely inclination, favoring much their worthy disposition, in hope thereby to advance the enlargement of Christian religion, to the glory of God Almighty. [1]

In 1629 King Charles I granted the Massachusetts Bay Charter that included the following sentence:

Where by our said people, inhabitants there, may be so religiously, peaceable and civilly governed as their good life and orderly conversation may win and incite the natives of the country to their knowledge and obedience of the only true God and Saviour of mankind, and the Christian faith, which in our royal

*intention and the adventurers free
profession, is the principal end of this
plantation.*[2]

The provisional government instituted
in Connecticut in 1638-39 prescribed
within its fundamental orders that the
government was formed to foster and
enlarge obedience to God and "the
preservation of the Christian religion."

Similar acknowledgments were made
in organizing Rhode Island in 1638. Its
founders signed a document containing
the following:

*We whose names are underwritten do
here solemnly in the presence of Jehovah
incorporate ourselves into a Bodie Politic
and as He shall help, will submit our
persons, lives and estates unto our Lord
Jesus Christ, the King of Kings and Lord
of Lords and to all those perfect and most
absolute laws of his given us in his holy
word of truth, to be guided and judged
thereby. Exodus 24:3, 4; II Chronicles
11:3; II Kings 11:17.*[3]

The Carolinas' Charter, signed in 1622
by King Charles, commended their
"laudable and pious zeal" and

acknowledged that the settlement was constituted for "the propagation of the Christian faith." It is even clearer that the settlement of the Quakers in Pennsylvania was for the establishment of religious freedom.

Obviously most of the original thirteen colonies were founded to insure Christian liberty. The dynamic that motivated these hardy pioneers to leave their homeland and endure the hardships of a new world was spiritual. Admittedly, many later came here to make their fortune, but the original documents prove that Bible-oriented Christians, for the most part, were the first ones to establish this land. The laws of the people were largely Bible laws, moral and social standards basically Christian. In fact, as unbelievable as it seems today, several of the early colonial constitutions actually required that any governmental office holder acknowledge personal belief in Jesus Christ before he could seek election.

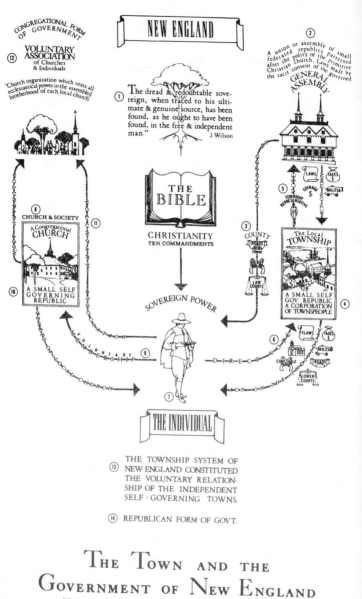

NEW ENGLAND

CONGREGATIONAL FORM OF GOVERNMENT

⑫ **VOLUNTARY ASSOCIATION** of Churches & Individuals

"Church organization which vests all ecclesiastical power in the assembled brotherhood of each local church"

① "The dread & redoubtable sovereign, when traced to his ultimate & genuine source, has been found, as he ought to have been found, in the free & independent man." J. Wilson

② A union or assembly of small federated republics patterned after the polity of the primitive Christian church. Laws made by the tacit consent of the governed

GENERAL ASSEMBLY

LAWS   TAXES

⑤ TOWNSHIP REPRESENTATIVE   COINAGE $ MILITIA

③ COUNTY   ROADS   TOWNS

THE BIBLE

CHRISTIANITY
TEN COMMANDMENTS

SOVEREIGN POWER

⑧ **CHURCH & SOCIETY**

A Congregational **CHURCH**

⑩ A SMALL SELF GOVERNING REPUBLIC

⑪

SELF LAW COURTS

The Local TOWNSHIP

④ A SMALL SELF GOV. REPUBLIC A CORPORATION OF TOWNSPEOPLE

⑥ BYLAWS   TAXES

SCHOOLS   MILITIA

CONSTABLE   ROADS

LOWER LAW COURTS

V-O-L-U-N-T-A-R-Y ⑨   M-E-M-B-E-R-S-H-I-P   I-N   C-H-U-R-C-H

D—I—R—E—C—T

On Treason Oath

⑦

THE INDIVIDUAL

⑬ THE TOWNSHIP SYSTEM OF NEW ENGLAND CONSTITUTED THE VOLUNTARY RELATIONSHIP OF THE INDEPENDENT SELF-GOVERNING TOWNS.

⑭ REPUBLICAN FORM OF GOVT.

THE TOWN AND THE GOVERNMENT OF NEW ENGLAND

MAYFLOWER COMPACT 1620 TO 1686 THE ARRIVAL OF GOV. ANDROS

The BIBLE, CHURCH, GOVERNMENT and the INDIVIDUAL

The relationship of the Bible to both church and government is portrayed in a unique chart (facing page) that depicts the New England concept of town and state government.[4]

For the first one hundred years and more of life in the Colonies, the Biblical standards of law and principles for living undergirded government, commerce, morality, religion, and almost every area of life. Many of the first government leaders and school teachers were ministers of the Gospel. In the passage of time these men overlooked the fact that a Governor is called a "minister of God" and gradually withdrew from government service and gave themselves exclusively to the propagation of the Gospel, much to the detriment of government. By this time the Colonies developed to such a degree that many settlers were attracted to the New World's promise of riches and freedom from political oppression. Slowly the pervading influence of Christians began to wane, and government started to fall into the hands of men who were not motivated by Jesus Christ or filled with Bible principles.

FREE THINKING HUMANISM

The age of enlightenment and the skepticism of the Frenchmen Voltaire and Rousseau helped to propagate the naturalism and deism that permeated England and spread to the Colonies. Political ambition, greed, and the natural result of libertine living had a catastrophic effect on the morals of western civilization. In fact, the tragedies which have plagued Central Europe for the past 175 years and ultimately embroiled America in two world wars can be traced directly to this "free thinking" humanism. Modern educators inundate the minds of our youth with the false notion that our freedom had its roots in the "enlightenment movement" of the French Revolution, but nothing could be further from the truth. As Dr. Peter F. Drucker wrote:

It cannot be denied that the

Enlightenment and the French Revolution contributed to the freedom of the nineteenth century. But their contribution was entirely negative. . . . On the contrary: the Enlightenment, the French Revolution, and their successors down to the rationalist Liberalism of our days, are in irreconcilable opposition to freedom. Fundamentally, rationalist Liberalism is totalitarian. . . .

There is a straight line from Rousseau to Hitler — a line that takes in Robespierre, Marx and Stalin.[5]

The evidence that naturalism and humanism were negative influences on society becomes readily apparent in their effect on France, ushering in the French Revolution which culminated in the "Reign of Terror." Dr. J. Wesley Bready sums it up in these words:

. . . "the Reign of Terror," when Paris gutters ran red with human blood; when a prostitute was crowned Goddess of Reason; and when each new champion of freedom, crying "Liberty, Equality and Fraternity," rushed his fellow champions to the guillotine, lest they rush him there first.[6]

From that day to this, France has not enjoyed a stable government for as long as one generation. Instead, she has struggled through three republics, one commune, and three empires, enduring the ignominious experience of having foreign troops invade her land in each successive generation. France is a nation that has abandoned God — and seemingly has been abandoned by God. During the same period of time, America turned back to God, has never been conquered by a foreign power, and has rescued France from foreign oppressors twice in the last sixty years.

The GREAT AWAKENING

Thirty-five years before the signing of the Declaration of Independence, God sent a man to England and America to change their destiny. At a time when honesty, morality, virtue, and church attendance were at an all-time low in the Colonies, Evangelist George Whitefield, with his booming, clear voice, came to America calling for her to "repent." He was followed by John Wesley and Francis Asbury. During the next twenty-five to thirty years a state of revival spread through the Colonies that prepared them for the titanic struggle for freedom that lay just ahead. Lest you think this an exaggeration, consider President Calvin Coolidge's later observation: "America was born in a revival of religion. Back of that revival were John Wesley, George Whitefield and Francis Asbury."[7]

No less an eye witness to the transformation of colonial life in that period was Benjamin Franklin.

It was wonderful to see the change soon made in the manners of our inhabitants. From being thoughtless or indifferent about religion, it seemed as if all the world were growing religious, so that one could not walk thro' the town in an evening without hearing psalms sung in different families of every street. [8]

It is almost impossible to exaggerate the influence on American education created by the preaching of Whitefield and Wesley. Harvard University, according to its president, Dr. Willard, was affected in the following manner:

That which forbodes the most lasting advantage is the new state of the college. Gentlemen's sons that were sent here only for a mere polite education, are now so full of zeal for the cause of Christ and the love of souls as to devote themselves absolutely to the study of divinity. The college is entirely changed; the students are full of God — and will I hope come out blessings to this and succeeding generations. [9]

Princeton University, originally called "the Log College," was a struggling institution when George Whitefield recognized the need to help it spiritually and financially. He raised money for it on both sides of the Atlantic, and today "no less than sixty-two American colleges trace their origin to 'the Log College'."[10] In 1914, the bicentennial of Whitefield's birth, a statue was erected at the University of Pennsylvania, acknowledging him as the "inspirer and original Trustee of the Charity School of 1740, the forerunner of the University of Pennsylvania, as he solicited the first donations to the Library of the University . . . guided the new school of learning by his godly counsel, heartened it by his masterful preaching, and inspired it with his noble life."[11]

With these facts in mind we can appreciate the statement of the British Prime Minister David Lloyd George:

I do not know the exact figures of Britain's debt to America, but I am told that it is a thousand million odd at the present moment. It is nothing to the debt that America owes us. Write on the balance sheet: Debtor, a thousand and ninety millions; Creditor — John Wesley and George Whitefield. [12]

Many years later General Douglas MacArthur wrote:

History fails to record a single precedent in which nations subject to moral decay have not passed into political and economic decline. There has been either a spiritual awakening to overcome the moral lapse, or a progressive deterioration leading to ultimate national disaster. [13]

Certainly this has proven true in the life of America several times, though not quite so dramatically as The Great Awakening. It was particularly necessary in preparing the proper moral climate for establishing on this continent "a new nation conceived in liberty."

The MINISTERS' INFLUENCE on EARLY AMERICAN HISTORY

One of the least known but easily substantiated facts of American history is the profound influence of ministers on the framing of our country, not only in early colonizations such as Rhode Island by Reverend Roger Williams, for religious freedom purposes, or in the revival known as The Great Awakening, but in the rallying of people to oppose England prior to the Revolutionary War.

It is difficult for us moderns to picture the days before television, radio, weekly news magazines, and daily papers when communication presented a serious problem. During such a time churchgoers comprised a much higher percentage of the population than they do today, and thus the pulpit provided a powerful influence on the masses of people. Critics of the revolutionary spirit beginning to form in the 1760's and 70's asserted that "the clergy and especially the Puritan clergy of New England were among the chief agitators of the revolution and, after it began, among the most zealous and successful in keeping it alive."[14]

Many ministers throughout the Colonies used their preaching services to educate the people in the field of political theory. They also interpreted special news events in the light of Bible teaching. From these ministers the lay people began to understand the Scriptural teachings regarding government which was of divine origin and for the good of man. Their emphasis on the freedom of the individual, the natural equality of all men, the power of the people as a collective body, the right to own and protect one's own property, the responsibility to provide for and protect one's own family, and the separation of church and state carried the ring of divine authority because these Bible-believing ministers used the Scriptures to verify their teachings. It is no wonder that such concepts ultimately found their way into the Constitution and the Bill of Rights.

In pre-revolutionary times, among the tools used to whip the populace into the spirit of revolt against England were the tracts, booklets, and articles passed freely among the people. What modern historians often fail to acknowledge is that many of these powerful writings were produced by ministers. Only a small percentage of the population was college-educated, and, since most ministers at that time were graduates of Harvard, Princeton, and Yale, they were among the few who were qualified to write such material. Their preaching was characterized by an evangelistic zeal, and their writings contained the same fiery appeal.

One of the difficult problems with which the God-fearing early Americans had to cope was the Biblical justification for revolting against Mother England. Who could better vindicate Christian consciences on this matter than the local man of God? He usually did so, using the Bible for his authority, by pointing out two fundamental facts:

1. *"A government that did not have the good of the people at heart did not have*

the sanction of God."[15]
2. Christians should be obedient to "the powers that be," and in this case the true power was the duly elected local and colonial government working in agreement with the other twelve Colonies. England and the King were presented as insensitive, greedy taskmasters whose self-interest was destructive of the liberty of the people. In such a climate Patrick Henry's ringing challenge, "Give me liberty or give me death," was considered a justifiable Christian position.

The Boston Massacre, which occurred in March of 1770, provides a good illustration of how deeply involved Bible-believing ministers were in exciting the populace. Reverend John Lathrop of the Old North Church, a graduate of Princeton, on the Sunday after the massacre preached a moving sermon entitled, "The Voice of Thy Brother's Blood Cryeth Unto Me From The Ground." In this sermon, published throughout the Colonies (and even in London), the people were challenged to abolish a government that was so obviously opposed to the good of the people and to replace it with another. His challenge was repeated by many other ministers throughout the Colonies — so much so that one opponent of the revolution commented that after the Boston Massacre "the pulpits rang their chimes upon blood guiltiness, in order to incite the people."[16]

The ministers' influence did not stop when the Revolutionary War began. They were among the first recruiters of troops; many who volunteered as chaplains were often known to pick up rifles at the sides of fallen comrades and use them in helping to repulse enemy attacks. One started a small ammunition plant that played a vital role in supplying much-needed musket shot, and others led through personal example by giving as much as a year's salary to the struggling government to help finance the war. It would be an overstatement to suggest that ministers were solely responsible for starting and winning the Revolutionary War, but it is no exaggeration to suggest that the revolution would not have enjoyed the widespread acceptance of the people nor their ultimate victory without the active influence of the ministers.

Space does not permit inclusion of the further influence of ministers in the Continental Congress, the settlement of the frontiers, their opposition to slavery, their defense of the government in all of its wars, and their many humanitarian enterprises. Even today ministers comprise the group at the forefront for Christian education and the establishment of Christian schools. If given enough time, the rapidly growing Christian school movement, I believe, will someday replace the atheistic education system as the primary source of future American leadership.

Without a doubt, Bible-motivated ministers have had a profound influence on the history of America.

The DECLARATION of INDEPENDENCE

It is not my intention to suggest that all the delegates to the Continental Congress from the thirteen Colonies were Christians. Clearly, however, the Christian principles taught in the Word of God influenced the writing of the Declaration of Independence. Consider the following selected statements:

. . . the Laws of Nature and of Nature's God entitle them . . . that they are endowed by their Creator with certain unalienable Rights . . . .

. . . We, therefore, the Representatives of the United States of America, in General Congress, Assembled, appealing to the Supreme Judge of the world for the rectitude of our intentions, do in the Name and by Authority of the good People of these Colonies, solemnly publish and declare, That these United

Colonies are, and of Right ought to be, FREE AND INDEPENDENT STATES; . . . And for the support of this Declaration, with a firm reliance on the protection of Divine Providence, we mutually pledge to each other our Lives, our Fortunes, and our sacred Honor.

But the dependence of God characterized by the above statements was not unique. Consider the first prayer offered in Congress by Reverend Jacob Duche:

O Lord, our Heavenly Father, high and mighty, King of kings, and Lord of Lords, who dost from Thy throne behold all the dwellers on earth, and reignest with power supreme and uncontrolled over all the Kingdoms, Empires and Governments; look down in mercy, we beseech Thee, on these our American States, who have fled to Thee from the rod of the oppressor, and thrown themselves on Thy gracious protection, desiring to be henceforth dependent only on Thee; to Thee have they appealed for the righteousness of their cause; to Thee do they now look up for that countenance and support, which Thou alone canst give; take them, therefore, Heavenly

Father, under Thy nurturing care; give them wisdom in Council and valor in the field; defeat the malicious designs of our cruel adversaries; convince them of the unrighteousness of their cause; and if they persist in their sanguinary purposes, O! let the voice of Thine own unerring justice, sounding in their hearts, constrain them to drop the weapons of war, from their unnerved hands in the day of battle! Be Thou present, O God of wisdom, and direct the councils of this honorable assembly; enable them to settle things on the best and surest foundation. That the scene of blood may be speedily closed; that order, harmony and peace may be effectually restored, and truth and justice, religion and piety, prevail and flourish amongst Thy people. Preserve the health of their bodies and vigor of their minds; shower down on them and the millions they here represent, such temporal blessings, as Thou seest expedient for them in this world, and crown them with everlasting glory in the world to come. All this we ask in the name and through the merits of Jesus Christ, Thy Son and our Savior. Amen. [17]

That the majority of our founding

fathers were not atheistic humanists but deeply God-conscious men is clearly manifest in their many public statements, from Benjamin Franklin to Patrick Henry. The man often referred to as the Father of our Country, President George Washington, in his first inaugural address, made his faith in God crystal clear:

It would be peculiarly improper to omit in this first official act my fervent supplications to that Almighty Being who rules over the universe, who presides in the councils of nations, and whose providential aids can supply every human defect, that His benediction may consecrate to the liberties and happiness of the people of the United States a Government instituted by themselves for these essential purposes, and may enable every instrument employed in its administration to execute with success the functions allotted to his charge. In tendering this homage to the Great Author of every public and private good, I assure myself that it expressed your sentiments not less than my own, nor those of my fellow-citizens at large less than either. No people can be bound to acknowledge and adore the Invisible Hand which conducts the affairs of men more than those of the United States. Every step by which they have advanced to the character of an independent nation seems to have been distinguished by some token of providential agency; and in the important revolution just accomplished in the system of their united government the tranquil deliberations and voluntary consent of so many distinct communities from which the event has resulted cannot be compared with the means by which most governments have been established without some return of pious gratitude, along with an humble anticipation of the future blessings which the past seems to presage . . .

The propitious smiles of Heaven can never be expected on a nation that disregards the eternal rules of order and right which Heaven itself has ordained; . . .

Having thus imparted to you my sentiments as they have been awakened by the occasion which brings us together, I shall take my present leave; but not without resorting once more to the benign

Parent of the Human Race in humble supplication that, since He has been pleased to favor the American people with opportunities for deliberating in perfect tranquility, and dispositions for deciding with unparalleled unanimity on a form of government for the security of their union and the advancement of this happiness, so His divine blessing may be equally conspicuous in the enlarged views, the temperate consultations, and the wise measures on which the success of this Government must depend.[18]

"The eternal rules of order and right" to which President Washington referred, kept this nation during the last two hundred years while it was tried severely in the War of 1812, a titanic civil war, two world wars, famines, and depressions. Today we face our greatest enemy, atheistic humanism, which seeks to destroy our moral character and divert us from the principles that have produced the greatest nation in the history of the world. These principles were not dreamed up by the genius of our forefathers; they are Biblical principles written into the Constitution because they characterized the thinking of the framers of our Constitution. Dean Manion, a lawyer, has stated it this way:

Look closely at these self-evident truths, these imperishable articles of American Faith upon which all our government is firmly based. First and foremost is the existence of God. Next comes the truth that all men are equal in the sight of God. Third is the fact of God's great gift of unalienable rights to every person on earth. Then follows the true and single purpose of all American Government, namely, to preserve and protect these God-made rights of God-made man. [19]

The BIBLE'S INFLUENCE on the CONSTITUTION

Not only does the Constitution recognize the existence of God (as already seen) and government's dependence on Him for authority to govern his fellow men, but it also recognizes the depravity of man. The most famous part of the Constitution, in my opinion, is the "check-and-balance system of government." In grade school we all learned about the three interdependent sections to our Government: (1) the Legislative Congress that makes our laws; (2) the Executive that administers them; and (3) the Judicial that is to guarantee that our government functions within the framework of the Constitution.

Have you ever wondered why these writers of our Constitution so divided the government? Because they understood the basic nature of man. Unlike modern atheistic humanists, who carry on a running romance with socialistic idealism, they did not believe that man is born neutral and influenced primarily by his environment. Rather, they were persuaded that man is corrupt, just as the Bible teaches: "The heart is deceitful and desperately wicked; who can know it?" (Jeremiah 17:9). For that reason our forefathers did not want a president who possessed absolute power, for they knew, as Lord Acton later said, "Power corrupts and absolute power corrupts absolutely." Failure to understand this principle causes humanistic man to yearn idealistically for a one-world governor or dictator who would guarantee world peace. Because he does not understand the nature of man, he does not realize that such peace would be secured at the expense of personal liberty.

Our forefathers made it clear that God grants liberty to man; therefore the government's job is to insure it by protecting him from foreign invasion and exploitation by his countryman. To do this he needs laws and someone to whom he must be accountable; hence, the "check-and-balance system."

The BIBLE'S INFLUENCE on the INDIVIDUAL

Individual freedom is one of the most treasured blessings of the American Constitution. Such freedom is really unique to America. Prior to that time dictators, kings, and monarchs controlled the destinies of their subjects. Not so in America! Instead, our Constitution recognizes that all men are created equal (meaning before the law). By contrast, humanism teaches collectivism — the individual doesn't matter; it's the mass that counts. The millions in China, India, and communist countries are thus viewed collectively. In America all men are entitled to the same rights. Where did such a notion come from? The Bible dealt with man as an individual with a free will to do as he chooses. But the greatest evidence of the unique importance of the individual is seen in John 3:16, "For God so loved the world, that He gave His only begotten Son, that whosoever believeth in Him should not perish but have everlasting life." Christ died, not for nations, but individuals. For two hundred years Americans have enjoyed unprecedented freedom as individuals, a concept derived from the Bible.

The BIBLE'S INFLUENCE on RESPONSIBILITY

One facet of our American heritage that the humanists like to ridicule today is what they term "the puritan work ethic." What they really mean is the principle that every adult is individually responsible for his own welfare, in contrast to the government's assuming that responsibility. Traditionally, Americans have accepted that Biblical truism, ". . . that if any would not work, neither should he eat." (II Thessalonians 3:10) Why? Because although most people would voluntarily carry "their own weight" in a communal style of life, there are always those few sluggards who take advantage of the industry of others and refuse to work. If the government steps in and subsidizes their inactivity through welfare checks or food stamps, it not only perpetuates the inactivity by nullifying their personal initiative, but it strips them of their self-respect.

From the beginning the Old Testament commanded man that he should "earn his bread by the sweat of his face." Like all of God's commands, this one cooperates with man's mental and physical well-being by motivating him to work. At one time America was noted for her "industrious people," but in recent years a humanistic philosophy has characterized our national leadership; consequently, we have the dubious paradox of enjoying the highest level of affluence on the one hand and the largest number of welfare recipients of any country in the world on the other.

The Bible is very specific on this matter. A healthy adult man is responsible to God for the care of his family. The Apostle Paul warned, "He that provideth not for his own house hath denied the faith and is worse than an infidel" (I Timothy 5:8). Many warnings in Scriptures are addressed to the "sluggard" who is even taught to take heed to the ant, the most industrious of creatures. The near bankruptcy of the city of New York because of fiscal irresponsibility and runaway welfarism would have been deemed impossible by the founders of our Constitution.

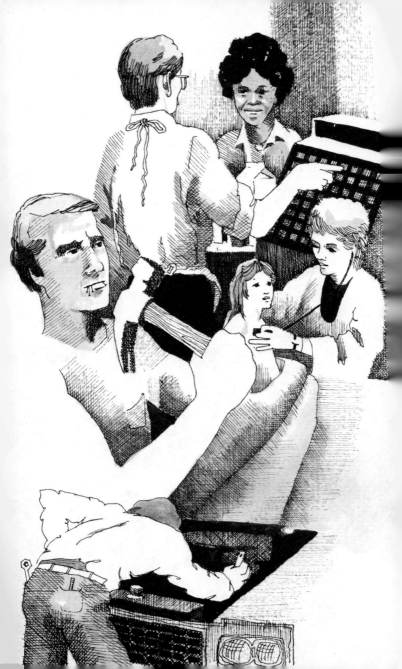

The BIBLE'S INFLUENCE on FREE ENTERPRISE

Free enterprise is a dirty word to many of our brainwashed college students who have been subjected to the idealism of their naive professors, who continually point out the evils of "capitalism" and extol the virtues of a government-controlled economy. The fact that socialism, the essence of such a controlled economy, has never worked in a single country where it has been tried does not discourage these intellectual termites from destroying the appreciation of our nation's youth for the most successful economic experiment in the history of the world. Exhibit "A" for socialism is Soviet Russia. Prior to 1914 the Crimea was referred to as "the breadbasket of the world." In good years they exported 25% of the world's wheat

Tim LaHaye

supply. Today, after sixty years of
communism and national socialism, they
cannot feed their own countrymen and
have to import millions of tons of free
enterprise American wheat.

It would be futile for me as a Christian
to deny the evils of capitalism in America.
Wherever sinful, fallen human beings
exist, evil abounds. But the best human
economy, as seen in both Testaments of
the Bible, establishes that some men own
property and hire laborers to whom they
pay a fair wage for services rendered. In
the early days of human history, God
approved the man who owned his own
land and possessions and condemned the
men who coveted "any thing that is thy
neighbor's." Jesus Christ used many
stories of "householders," "landowners,"
and their "servants" or employees who
worked for them. He commended the
wise investment of one's "talents," giving
the greatest approval to the man who
earned the greatest increase. In Ephesians
6 the Apostle Paul gave instructions to the
Spirit-filled employee with the awareness
that God is watching and we are all equal
before him.

The right of private ownership of land is

seemingly written intuitively on the mind of man, for universally every man wants to own his home. The greatest enemy of private ownership is dictatorial government, for in depriving man of his possessions or the potential of owning his own property, it strips man of his greatest source of motivation. For all the admitted evils of many people operating within it, free enterprise is still the best economic system the world has ever known as far as producing the greatest good for the largest number of people. It offers more for less effort, and it has the unique advantage of providing its own inherent check-and-balance arrangement through its competitive feature. Socialism, by contrast, is non-competitive. It concentrates all economic power in a small elite group of "planners," who themselves are evil. Historically, free enterprise in America has broken the yoke of concentrated, undivided economic power, unleashed an avalanche of creativity and productivity, produced the highest standard of living ever known, and founded the greatest missionary and evangelistic effort of all time.

The BIBLE'S INFLUENCE on CIVIL SAFETY

Among the tragedies of contemporary life is the fact that our streets are no longer safe for law-abiding citizens, particularly at night. Washington, D.C., New York, and Atlanta, Georgia, are apparently vying for the dubious honor of being the most dangerous cities in the world. The maudlin sentimentality of humanists that idealistically produces a lenient attitude towards criminals is maintained at the expense of law-abiding citizens. By no stretch of the imagination can this policy be laid at the door of the Christian community, nor was it the plan of the framers of our Constitution.

The Bible instructs man not to steal, rape, and kill and entrusts to government the responsibility of just punishment if he disobeys. The Biblical principle, "an eye for an eye," has been ridiculed by the intellectual community until secretaries in the nation's capital have to be escorted to and from their cars to federal buildings by armed guards. This was never the case when our government followed the traditionally American policies derived from Scripture. Discredit it all they may, social experimenters will never improve on the capital punishment principle clearly taught in the Scriptures and practiced in our country during the days when America was a safe country in which to live. As unpleasant as it is for government to take the life of a proven criminal, it is an improvement over setting him free to kill other innocent victims. Our streets will become increasingly unsafe unless we return to the responsible practice of dealing with criminals as laid out in the Scriptures.

The BIBLE'S INFLUENCE on EDUCATION

Nowhere is the influence of the Bible and Christianity more apparent than in the field of education. When the Pilgrims came to America, free schools for every man's child were unknown. Throughout Europe it was customary only for the offspring of the rich and nobles, and select gifted children, to receive an education. In their quest for religious freedom and because the King James Bible had been translated into English just a few years before they sailed to the New World, most parents desired that their children learn to read, primarily so they could read the Bible.

Many of the first school teachers were ministers of the Gospel, for most were college graduates before emigrating to America; furthermore, the church building provided the ideal meeting place. Often the "one room school house" was really the local church building. Naturally, these men of God trained their young students in Biblical principles.

Christians have always been interested in education. Consequently, the earliest schools and colleges in this new land were founded by Christians. We have already noted the impact of The Great Awakening on education during the eighteenth century. You will be interested to know that Harvard College (the present-day Harvard University) was founded in 1636 by the Reverend John Harvard. The first pamphlet published by any American college was printed in London for Harvard College in 1643. In this 26-page booklet describing the college the preamble states,

After God had carried us safe to New England and we had convenient places for God's worship, and settled the civil government, one of the things we longed for and looked for was to advance learning and perpetuate it to posterity. And dreading to leave an illiterate ministry to the churches whenever our present ministry shall lie in the dust, and as we were thinking and consulting how to effect this great work, it pleased God to stir up the heart of one Mr. Harvard, a godly gentleman and a lover of learning then living amongst us, to give us the one-half of his estate and all of his library for this purpose. [20]

After the preamble they listed the admission rules of the college. Consider the first two:

When any scholar is able to understand Cicero or such like Latin authors extempore and can speak true Latin in verse and prose and decline perfectly the paradigms of nouns and verbs in the Greek tongue, let him then and not before be capable of admission to the college . . . [21]

Obviously they had high entrance requirements.

Let every student be plainly instructed and earnestly pressed to consider well the main end of his life and studies to know God and Jesus Christ which is eternal life (John 17:3); and therefore to lay Christ in the bottom as the only foundation of all

sound knowledge and learning; and
seeing the Lord only giveth wisdom, let
every one seriously set himself by prayer
in secret to seek it of him (Proverbs 2:3). [22]

There can be no question that Harvard
College was originally founded for the
purpose of training young people to serve
Jesus Christ.

Someone has pointed out that all the
colleges in this country during the first one
hundred years of our history were
founded by churches, denominations, or
religious groups. Certainly that was the
case of Harvard, Yale (1701), and
Princeton (1746). That is significant
because these three colleges were the
headquarters for preparing school
teachers until World War I.

Teachers trained in these schools could
be expected to inculcate Bible principles
into the minds of their students so that
even though Americans were not
overwhelmingly Christian, they were not
unfamiliar with Biblical principles for
living.

Unfortunately, Columbia University
gradually replaced these colleges in the
preparation of school teachers until today

most teachers' colleges have been
influenced by graduates of Columbia.
This, plus the humanistic influence of
progressive education has taken over the
public school until the Bible is now the
only unwelcome book on the campuses it
produced. In our bicentennial year the
once great American school system has
become a massive indoctrination center
whose leaders seem bent on producing
radical activists so dissatisfied with the
American system that they would
overthrow it by force and violence if they
could. Today's schools are so godless,
immoral, drug-ridden, unsafe, and in
many cases sub-par educationally that
they are no longer acceptable to many
parents. Consequently the Christian
schools that offer a thorough but
Biblically-oriented education comprise
the fastest growing movement in the
country. Churches that have been sound
asleep on education for several
generations and have allowed the public
schools to do their job for them are
awakening to the fact that we have a
responsibility both to God and our
country to educate our nation's children.

The BIBLE'S INFLUENCE on CULTURE

Time will not permit us to cover in detail the profound influence of the Bible on art, music, and literature. Some of the most beautiful paintings were inspired by Bible stories, as were many of the novels, poems, and literary masterpieces. Even some of the works of non-Christian writers and painters in the United States contained Biblical principles. This is in marked contrast to the wild art that goes under the guise of "impressionism," the loud beat "music" with its desolate and often mournful laments, and the pornography that is so frequently dubbed "literature." "Freedom of the press" and "freedom of speech" were never intended by our Biblically-oriented forefathers to constitute a license to destroy the minds and corrupt the morals of today's youth.

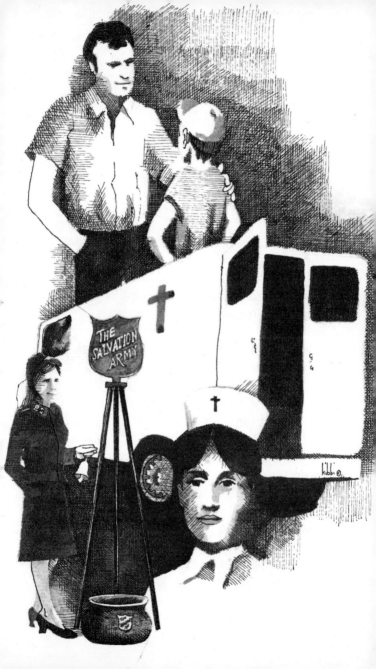

The BIBLE'S INFLUENCE on HUMANITARIANISM

Our Lord's command to "love thy neighbor as thyself" has always been a hallmark of true Christianity. Consequently, Christian people as individuals or as groups founded many orphanages, hospitals, and humanitarian organizations that have provided relief for millions of our countrymen. The Salvation Army was originated by a godly minister, General William Booth; the Red Cross was established by a Christian lady named Clara Barton in 1881; the Young Men's Christian Association and the Young Women's Christian Association were founded as a result of a prayer meeting. Who can estimate the good these organizations accomplished in their early years? It is safe to say that until the turn of this century most of the humanitarian and philanthropic organizations known in this country were established by Christians. To this day I do not know of a hospital, orphanage, or old people's home instituted by atheists. A Biblical principle teaches our countrymen to "do unto others as you would have them do unto you."

Have you ever tried to imagine what America would be like if all Christian and Bible influence were removed? What would we have left? The ugliest kind of twentieth century barbarism, resembling the inhumanity perpetuated in Nazi Germany or Russia and China since the war. When the deification of man is substituted for God as the source of man's hope, the result inevitably fashions the stifling economy of socialism, the cruel government of communism that has already murdered over 40 million people (some authorities estimate this tragic "population deficit" at 73,000,000), and the loss of individual freedom. Two-thirds of the world today is enslaved in communism and socialism. America is the human hope of the world, and Jesus Christ is the hope of America. Our present weakness, confusion, bureaucracy, immorality, and other national evils cannot be traced to the Bible or Christians but to the subversive erosion of basic Christian principles that have made this the greatest nation under God that the world has ever known. Unless we return to the Bible principles that provided our nation's greatness, we will pass like others before us.

A SENATOR'S VIEW of AMERICAN HERITAGE

Senator Robert Byrd of West Virginia, a Bible teacher and respected member of the U.S. Legislature, was so moved by the disastrous Supreme Court decision of June 25, 1962, declaring prayer in schools unconstitutional, that he delivered the following address to his colleagues. The superb content of this speech, taken from pages 11002-11004 of the Congressional Record of June 27, 1962, should be read by every American, for this noted political leader clearly delineates the powerful influence of the Bible, belief in God, and the Christian faith on the history of America.

Mr. President, Thomas Jefferson expressed the will of the American majority, in 1776, when he included in the Declaration of Independence the statement that "all men are endowed by their Creator with certain unalienable rights, that among these are life, liberty, and the pursuit of happiness."

Little could Mr. Jefferson suspect, when he penned that line, that the time would come when the Nation's highest court would rule that a nondenominational prayer to the Creator, if offered by school children in the public schools of America during class periods, is unconstitutional . . . .

Wherever one may go in this great National City, he is constantly reminded of the strong spiritual awareness of our forefathers who wrote the Federal Constitution, who built the schools and churches, who hewed the forests, dredged the rivers and the harbors, fought savages, and created a republic.

In no other place in the United States are there so many, and such varied official evidences of deep and abiding faith in God on the part of Government as there are in Washington . . . .

A visitor entering Washington by train sees the words of Christ prominently inscribed above the main arch leading into Union Station. Here at the very entrance to the seat of Government of the

United States are the words:

**"The truth shall make you free"
(John 8:32).**

Nearby is another inscription cut into enduring stone, the words from the Eighth Psalm of the Old Testament:

"Thou has put all things under His feet."

A third inscription reiterates the spiritual theme:

"Let all the end thou aimest at be thy country's, thy God's, and truth's."

All three inscriptions acknowledge the dependence of our Republic upon the guiding hand of Almighty God . . . .

The visitor to the Library of Congress may see a quotation from the Old Testament which reminds each American of his responsibility to his Maker. It reads:

"What doth the Lord require of thee, but to do justly and love mercy and to walk humbly with God?" (Micah 6:8).

Another Scriptural quotation prominently displayed in the lawmakers' library preserves the Psalmist's acknowledgement that all nature reflects the order and beauty of the Creator.

"The heavens declare the glory of God, and the firmament showeth His

handiwork." (Psalms 19:1).

Underneath the statue of History in the Library of Congress are Tennyson's prophetic lines:

"One God, one law, one element
And one far-off divine event,
To which the whole creation moves."

Additional proof that American national life is God centered comes from this Library of Congress inscription:

"The light shineth in the darkness, and the darkness comprehendeth it not" (John 1:5).

On the east hall of the second floor of the Library of Congress, an anonymous inscription assures all Americans that they do not work alone —

"For a web begun God sends thread."

One of the most hallowed documents in the Nation's Capital is the Declaration of Independence, to which I have already alluded. It contains the basic philosophy of our Government, according to which God is the source of our rights. The original document can be seen by Americans visiting in Washington from throughout the 50 States of the Union.

One of the most impressive and beautiful sights in the Capital City is the Washington Monument rising above the city. When it was being built, citizens and organizations were permitted to donate blocks of stone containing inscriptions and from the top of the monument, one may read three Biblical quotations on the 24th landing. One, donated by the Methodist Church of New York, reads:

"The memory of the just is blessed" (Proverbs 22:6).

The Sunday School children of the Methodist Church of Philadelphia contributed a stone bearing the inscription:

"Train up a child in the way he should go, and when he is old, he will not depart from it" (Proverbs 22:6).

The third stone bears these words of Christ:

"Suffer the little children to come unto me and forbid them not, for of such is the kingdom of heaven" (Luke 18:16) . . . .

The city of Boston placed a stone slab on the 15th landing, on which appear the words:

"Sicut patribus sit Deus nobis. (As

*God was to our fathers, may He be
unto us.)"*

Baltimore's contribution, at the 12th
level, reads:

*"May heaven to this Union its
beneficence."*

The Indiana Lodge of Odd Fellows
contributed a stone on the sixth landing
which reads:

"In God we trust."

The United Sons of America provided
a stone bearing the inscription:

"God and Nature's land."

Near the Washington Monument is the
Lincoln Memorial, the Nation's tribute to
its martyred Civil War President. This
massive shrine pays homage to the
greatness of a simple and heroic man
whose very life was offered on the altar of
liberty. The gentleness, power, and
determination of Lincoln came to us
clearly through the features chiseled in
granite by the sculptor. We can almost
hear Lincoln speak the words which are
cut into the wall by his side:

*"That this Nation, under God, shall
have a new birth of freedom, and that
government of the people, by the
people, for the people, shall not perish*

from the earth."

In his second inaugural address, the great President made use of the words "God," "Bible," "providence," "Almighty," and "divine attributes."

Then his address continues:

"As was said 3,000 years ago so it still must be said, 'The judgments of the Lord are true and righteous altogether.'

"With malice toward none, with charity for all, with firmness in the right as God gives us to see the right let us strive on to finish the work we are in, to bind up the Nation's wounds, to care for him who shall have borne the brunt of battle and for his widow and his orphan — to do all which may achieve and cherish a just and lasting peace among ourselves and with all nations."

On the walls of the Jefferson Memorial which stands at the south end of the Tidal basin, are inscribed Jefferson's words:

"I have sworn upon the altar of God eternal hostility against every form of tyranny over the mind of men."

On a panel near the statue we find in Jefferson's words a forceful and explicit warning that to remove God from this country will destroy it. Here he says:

"God who gave us life gave us liberty. Can the liberties of a nation be secure when we have removed a conviction that these liberties are the gift of God? Indeed I tremble for my country when I reflect that God is just, that his justice cannot sleep forever. Commerce between master and slave is despotism. Nothing is more certainly written in the book of fate than that these people are to be free. Establish the law for educating the common people. This it is the business of the state to effect and on a general plan."

Jefferson foresaw that time would change conditions in this country, but he believed in the unchanging truth which would persist through any age. He held that the dignity of man came not from man himself, but from God. His memorial in our Nation's Capital is a constant reminder that respect for men is based upon his close affinity with God.

Let us reflect for a moment on the fact that Washington, Jefferson, Lincoln — the giants of America — had this in common: They all paid repeated tribute to this Nation's dependence upon God.

Benjamin Franklin, at the Constitutional Convention in 1787, stood to his feet one day, the oldest man in that illustrious gathering, and addressed the chair, in which sat General George Washington. Franklin said:

"Sir, I have lived a long time; and the longer I live, the more convincing proofs I see that God still governs in the affairs of men. If a sparrow cannot fall to the ground without our Father's notice, is it possible that we can build an empire without our Father's aid? I believe the Sacred Writings, which say that: Except the Lord build the house, they labor in vain that build it."

Franklin went on to move that a member of the clergy be invited to participate in the meetings from day to day, that they might invoke the wisdom and the guidance of the Father of Lights:

"Else," *he said,* **"we shall succeed no better than did the builders of Babel."**

Here was a real man; here was a statesman; here was an inventor; here was a philosopher; a man who had served his country; a wise man who had faith in a higher power; who had the courage to express that faith.

*Our country's truly great men —
Lincoln, Jefferson, Washington, Franklin,
Wilson, Robert E. Lee, and I need not
name others — these gigantic pillars of
strength in the structure of American
history were men who believed in a
Higher Power, and they had the courage
to express that belief in their words, their
writings, and their deeds.*

SUPREME COURT

*In the U.S. Supreme Court, the highest
court in the land, can be seen ample
evidence that our courts are conducted
according to belief in the Almighty. Thus
we find in the Supreme Court tribunal
such phrases as "divine inspiration,"
"truth," "safeguard of the rights of the
people," "defense of human rights," and
"liberty and peace."*

AT THE PENTAGON

*Just outside of Washington we find the
Pentagon, the world's largest office
building, and the center of the American
armed services. Flanking the main
entrance are two signs which read:*

"Worship daily according to your

faith."

Catholic, Protestant, and Jewish religious services are held at the Pentagon, and members of the three faiths are urged to attend.

The military leaders, too, recognize the necessity for strong spiritual training. General of the Army Omar Bradley said:

"This country has many men of science, too few men of God. It has grasped the mystery of the atom, but rejected the Sermon on the Mount."

As a lifetime soldier who has seen countless thousands of young Americans in uniform, he further observed:

"This shocking apathy to the conditions of their schools and the sterility of the curriculum is responsible even today for the political immaturity, the economic ignorance, the philosophical indifference, and the spiritual insolvency of so many young men . . . ."

Inasmuch as our greatest leaders have shown no doubt about God's proper place in the American birthright, can we, in our day, dare to do less? . . .[23]

This message by Senator Byrd and the

previous remarks barely scratch the surface in amassing evidence to prove how incisive has been the Bible's influence on American history. It is no wonder that many people of the world have referred to America as "A Christian nation," not because she is truly Christian, but because of the overriding influence of Christian concepts and influences that came out of the Bible.

IS THERE HOPE for AMERICA?

In a day when vain human reason stalks the school system, government-induced socialism in the guise of liberalism is raping the American free enterprise system, human initiative is being sapped by welfarism, the morals of our nation have dropped to an all time low, crime threatens our personal safety, and the liberal media is seeking to control the thinking of our people. A recent Gallup Poll indicates that loss of confidence in our system of government increases in direct proportion to the number of years a student remains in college. Many are asking, "is there any hope for America?"

My answer is an unqualified "Yes!" — the same hope the Pilgrims had when overwhelmed by severe winters in a new land; the same hope thinking Christians possessed before The Great Awakening;

the same hope that brought the spiritual revivals under Moody and Finney in the discouraging post-Civil War days. Yes, there is hope for America — it is a Holy Spirit-sent revival! Such a revival would bring our nation back to the principles that made this country great in the first place, the principles of God found in the Bible.

On every hand I see signs that lead me to believe it could well happen in the next few years. Consider some of these signs.

SOME SIGNIFICANT SIGNS of REVIVAL

1. A significant rise in the reading and studying of the Bible. Although the Bible has always been the best-selling book in America, with the increasing availability of new translations, versions, and helps, we are experiencing an unprecedented sale and use of Bibles.

2. A vital growth in many Bible-believing churches throughout the nation.

3. The booming sale of Bible-oriented books — not only in Christian bookstores, but on secular bookstands. One best-selling Christian book has hit a record of seven million copies, and others are following suit.

4. A recognition of the futility of humanistic solutions for moral and social problems and a willingness to consider Christianity's alternatives.

5. The booming Christian school

movement, causing millions of American parents to turn from the morally and philosophically bankrupt public schools, where tuition is free, and to send their children to Christian schools, where the tuition is paid at great personal sacrifice.

6. The increasing willingness of Christians to get involved in government as candidates for office and others ready to promote Christians for such office.

7. The tremendous number of Spirit-filled Christians, probably the largest in the history of America, who know how to effectively share their faith (and their number is growing).

WHAT CAN BE DONE?

Several things can be done to save our country:

1. Pray earnestly and effectively — II Chronicles 7:14.

2. Repent of our personal and national sins, bringing revival to our land. Too often "revival" is perceived to mean evangelism and personal piety as ends-in-themselves, with no real impact following in terms of shoe-leather Christianity. Merely *personal* Christianity is not *Biblical* Christianity at all. A personal Spirit-filled life followed by dynamic service and action in all areas of life, including education, politics, etc., is *Biblical* Christianity.

3. Ministers lead their churches in aggressive soulwinning and outreach programs, using television, radio, and the printed page to win millions of our countrymen to Christ and then ground them thoroughly in the Word of God so

that they can win others to influence our society back to God.

4. Create locally-controlled Christian school systems in every city of America to train future leaders thoroughly conversant with Biblical principles of individual freedom and responsibility and prepare them for governmental leadership with integrity.

5. Influence our society back to God through active participation in civic affairs. Christians, including ministers, should become politically active in election years so that Christians can be elected to school boards, city councils, and all other local, state, and national offices of the land, much as they were in the early days of our country. It has been pointed out by several Christian Congressmen, that we Christians comprise the largest voting block in America (estimated to be thirty to forty million) but we are almost totally disorganized. Consequently, we exercise little or no influence on our society. We need a massive number of Christians to step forward, to become precinct workers, block captains, and political candidates. Many nationally known key Christian leaders believe that if enough

Christians can be motivated to participate in future elections candidates for political office can develop a winning formula for electing Christian candidates who will return the sanity of Christian principles back into government.*

6. Build a television and press network that is committed to morality, decency, Americanism, and objective news reporting in accord with the traditions of America, in contrast to the present liberal ideologies that dominate the communications media.

7. Ministers must increasingly reach and teach the unadulterated Word of God to their congregations and through the printed page continue to reach the masses of our brainwashed society with their message.

The early American adage is still true — "the pen is mightier than the sword."

8. Ministers must once again become politically active in their local communities, motivating many Christians

---

For further information on how to become trained and effective in your community, write: The Institute for Christian Freedom, P.O. Box 1299, El Cajon, California 92022. Additional recommended reading: "One Nation Under God" by Russ Walton.

to become spiritually and Biblically active as outlined above and through their teaching raise up future Christian leaders who, when elected, will lead our country back to the Biblical concepts of church, state, individual, and government, that built this once-great nation.

We are indebted to many Christian and Bible-influenced patriots for the first two hundred years of our country's history. The next two hundred years, should Jesus tarry, could well depend on you!

FOOTNOTES

[1] **James M. Wheeler,** *The United States A Christian Nation* (Ft. Worth, Texas: The Mannly Co., 1955), p. 24.

[2] *Ibid.,* p. 25.

[3] *Ibid.,* p. 26.

[4] **Verna Hall and Rosalie Slater,** *Christian History of the Constitution of the United States* (San Francisco, California, 1960), p. 270C.

[5] **Verne Paul Kaub,** *Collectivism Challenges Christianity* (Winona Lake, Indiana: Light and Life Press, 1946), p. 48.

[6] *Ibid.,* p. 216.

[7] **John A. Stormer,** *The Death of a Nation* (Florissant, Missouri: The Liberty Bell Press, 1968), p. 129.

[8] *Ibid.,* p. 130.

[9] *Ibid.*

[10] **J. W. Bready,** *This Freedom — Whence?* (Winona Lake, Indiana: Light and Life Press, 1950), p. 312.

[11] *Ibid.,* pp. 312-313.

[12] *Ibid.,* p. 352.

[13] **Alice M. Baldwin,** *The New England Clergy*

and the American Revolution (New York: Frederick Ungar Publishing Co., 1958), p. XI.

14*Ibid.,* p. 23.

15*Ibid.,* p. 113.

16**Stormer,** p. 128.

17From "The First Prayer in Congress," offered by **Rev. Jacob Duche** before the First Continental Congress, on September 7, 1774, compliments of Bicentennial Specialities, P.O. Box 1072, La Mesa, California 92041.

18**Dan Smoot,** *The Dan Smoot Report,* 8, No. 29 (1962), 231-232.

19**Kaub,** p. 58.

20**Clyde J. Kennedy,** "America's Christian Heritage," *Christian Beacon,* June 29, 1961, p. 3.

21*Ibid.*

22*Ibid.*

23**"Senator Robert Byrd,** West Virginia, Outlined Before U.S. Senate, The Place of Prayer in National Life, 'The Supreme Court Decision Respecting Prayer in the Public Schools, ' " *Western Voice,* Aug. 9, 1962, p. 3.

ABOUT the AUTHOR

OUR CHRISTIAN HERITAGE . . . these words echo the concern that Tim LaHaye has for America's return to its Christian genesis. He believes revival in America is at hand, and actively supports Christians in government, recognizing that today as never before positions of leadership in America should be filled by Christian men and women.

DR. TIM LAHAYE . . . is the founder and president of Christian Heritage College now in its sixth year, with over 300 students. The college is destined to become a major Christian college on the west coast within the next 10 years.

. . . attended Moody Bible Institute in 1944, and was graduated from Bob Jones University with a B.A. degree in Bible in 1950. In 1962 Bob Jones University conferred on him an honorary doctorate in recognition of his pastoral

ministry and growing Bible conference
work with its emphasis on prophecy and
family living.

. . . has been a counselor and lecturer
for more than 27 years.

. . . is the author of national best sellers.

. . . is the senior pastor of two dynamic
churches, Scott Memorial Baptist (East)
and Scott Memorial Baptist (West) in El
Cajon and San Diego, California.

. . . in 1972 founded and became
president of Family Life Seminars, a
national family ministry holding seminars
in 75 major cities in the United States and
Canada, and in preparation conducts
counseling seminars for ministers to share
techniques found to be effective through
individual counseling of over 4,000
people during his 27 years as a pastor.

It is timely that Tim LaHaye should
write a book dealing with "The Bible's
Influence On American History."